Ancient Roman Homes

Brian Williams

Heinemann Library
Chicago, Illinois

© 2003 Reed Educational & Professional Publishing
Published by Heinemann Library,
an imprint of Reed Educational & Professional Publishing,
Chicago, Illinois

Customer Service 888-454-2279
Visit our website at www.heinemannlibrary.com

Designed by Tinstar Design
Illustrated by Jeff Edwards
Originated by Ambassador Litho
Printed by Wing King Tong in Hong Kong, China

07 06 05 04 03
10 9 8 7 6 5 4 3 2 1

Library of Congress Cataloging-in-Publication Data

Williams, Brian, 1943-
  Ancient Roman homes / Brian Williams.
      v. cm. -- (People in the past)
Includes bibliographical references and index.
Contents: City on the hills -- The Roman family -- The family at home -- Family worship -- Death in the family -- Life in the big city -- A Roman town -- Country life -- A ruler's palace -- Furniture and decoration -- Heat and light -- Clothes and hair -- Washing and bathing -- The kitchen -- The garden -- The baths and gymnasium -- Roman holiday -- Studying Roman homes.
  ISBN 1-58810-631-4 (lib. binding) -- ISBN 1-40340-519-0 (pbk.)
 1. Dwellings--Rome--Juvenile literature. 2. Architecture, Domestic--Rome--Juvenile literature. 3. Family--Rome--Juvenile literature. 4. Rome--Social life and customs--Juvenile literature. [1. Dwellings--Rome--History. 2. Rome--Social life and customs. 3. Rome--Civilization.] I. Title. II. Series.
  DG90 .W55 2002
  937--dc21
                              2002005713

Acknowledgments

The author and publishers are grateful to the following for permission to reproduce copyright material: pp. 5, 28, 31, 37, 38, 39, 40 John Seely; pp. 8, 10, 11, 12, 14, 16, 19, 20, 25, 26, 34, 41 Ancient Art & Architecture Collection; p. 13 Trevor Clifford; pp. 22, 23, 27 Terry Griffiths & Magnet Harlequin; pp. 24, 30, 32, 35, 42 AKG Photo London; p. 36 Museum of London; p. 43 Art Directors & TRIP.

Cover photograph by Scala Art Resource.

Every effort has been made to contact copyright holders of any material reproduced in this book. Any omissions will be rectified in subsequent printings if notice is given to the publisher.

Some words are shown in bold, **like this.** You can find out what they mean by looking in the glossary.

Contents

City on the Hills

Who were the Romans? To us today, they are probably the most famous of all ancient peoples. The Romans dated their history from the founding of their city, Rome, in 753 B.C.E. Over the centuries they built one of the great **empires** in history.

The Romans lived in Italy. Their city of Rome, built on seven hills, was the center of the Roman Empire. For a time, Rome was the biggest city in the world. There are many reminders of Roman times, because wherever they conquered, the Romans built roads and towns. From Britain in the west, to Turkey in the east, the remains of Roman walls, roads, and buildings can be seen. Much more lies buried beneath fields, and underneath the streets of modern cities.

This map shows the Roman world in 100 C.E., when the empire was at its biggest. In many lands, families under Roman rule copied Roman ways, and lived in Roman-style homes.

The first Roman homes

The first Romans were farmers who lived in a region called Latium, in central Italy. Families built their own homes, which were **thatched** huts grouped in villages beside the Tiber River. Later, the Romans built finer and longer-lasting houses of stone, brick, and **plaster.** They had tiled roofs, and were not unlike some of the older houses a visitor to Italy might see today. The villages grew into a great city, Rome.

Homes and families

The home was the center of Roman family life. The Romans believed that special gods looked after their homes. Not all people in the Roman world, however, were free to run their own lives or own homes. Many were **slaves.** Slaves lived in their owner's home, store, or farm, but few enjoyed many home comforts.

Rich and poor families lived very different lives. While poor people lived in small cottages or overcrowded apartments, rich families lived in wonderful country **villas** and town houses. We know about some Roman homes from Roman **sites**, such as towns, country villas, and army forts, uncovered by **archaeologists.** The most remarkable of these sites are Pompeii and Herculaneum in Italy, two towns buried by the erupting volcano Vesuvius in 79 CE. In this book, you will discover what Roman homes were like.

Sites like Pompeii, shown here, have provided lots of evidence of what Roman homes were like.

The Family Home

Roman homes ranged from small to magnificent. It all depended on how rich a person was. A few noble families were very rich and powerful. Such a family might own several homes—a town house in the city, and one or more farms in the countryside. They often also had a vacation home beside the sea, where the family went to escape the heat of the city in summer.

Roman merchants, storekeepers, and craftworkers often lived in the heart of the city, behind or above their shops and workshops. Wealthy **citizens** with good jobs, such as lawyers, doctors, and city officials, lived in nice town houses.

What a Roman house was like

A typical Roman house was four-sided, with two floors. The family bedrooms and the **slaves'** rooms were upstairs. Downstairs rooms included the *triclinium* or dining room, the *tablinum* or reception room, bathroom (not all homes had bathrooms), toilet, kitchen, and storerooms. The walls were made of stone or brick, with a tiled roof.

There were few windows on the outside, facing the street. All the rooms faced inwards, as can be seen from the remains of the Surgeon's House and other homes at Pompeii. The center of the house was the *atrium*, or main hall, open to the sky but sheltered from the rain by a sloping roof. Rainwater drained off the roof into a tank or pool. Around the *atrium*, doors or curtains opened into smaller ground floor rooms. At the back was an open sunny yard, with a shady walkway, the *peristyle*, and perhaps a fountain.

Clues to ownership

Evidence found in the remains of Roman houses gives us clues as to who lived there. In Pompeii, the house of Trebius Valens has the owner's name on an **inscription** in one bedroom. In another room was a collection of glass bottles for ointments and jewels, which shows this was probably the bedroom of the owner's wife.

The back of the house was the family's private space. The front of the house was the business area. In the *tablinum*, which was the public main living room, visitors were welcomed before moving into the *triclinium* to enjoy food and wine. Romans liked to be able to see the garden from the dining room. The Vettii brothers, wealthy merchants who lived in Pompeii, had several dining rooms to catch the sunlight at different seasons of the year. In the *atrium* of their house, the careful Vettii also had two safes for valuables.

Apartment buildings

Poorer people lived in rented apartments, in buildings two or three floors high. In Rome itself, some were as high as six floors. Many buildings were poorly built and overcrowded. From city records and the writings of residents, we know that the city firefighters, known as *vigiles*, were often called out to tackle fires in flimsy wooden buildings. More substantial houses lasted hundreds of years, and were homes to generations of Romans.

In the Roman town house, the opening in the roof let in daylight to the *atrium*. Rainwater was collected in the pool or *impluvium*. Front rooms were sometimes used as stores.

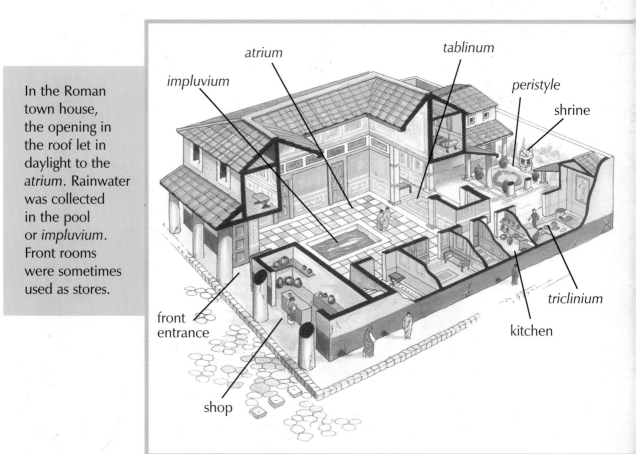

atrium

tablinum

impluvium

peristyle

shrine

front entrance

triclinium

kitchen

shop

The Roman Family

The Romans believed that the family and the family home were the rock on which their society was built. Young people were expected to marry and raise their children as good Romans.

The government played little part in home life. Marriages were arranged between families, and the wedding itself was held at home. Parents took on the responsibility of feeding, clothing, and also educating their children. There was no government aid for poor people, so they and their children went hungry when times were bad.

Father's out, mother's in charge

In a Roman family, a mother had charge of her small children until they went to school, at around the age of seven. Men went out to work. Women looked after the home: cleaning, preparing meals, **spinning,** and **weaving.** The hardest and dirtiest jobs in the home were usually done by **slaves,** both men and women. Many Roman houses had passageways so that slaves could move around without disturbing their master and his family in the family rooms.

A memorial stone carving, from the 2nd century B.C.E., shows a Roman family. Most Roman parents wanted large families, but many babies died.

Slave labor

Historians estimate that of around 6 to 7 million people in Roman Italy in the 1st century BCE, as many as 3 million were slaves. Rome's slave workers came from all over Europe, Africa, and the Middle East. Some were born slaves. Others were kidnapped by pirates and slave-traders, or were captured by the Roman army. Many slaves worked for the state or on farms. House-slaves were probably the luckiest—if they were owned by a kind master and mistress. Their work in the home—cooking, cleaning, gardening, and taking care of the children—was easier than digging ditches, clearing drains, or sawing timber.

Though a few rich women enjoyed a life of luxury at home, waited on by slaves, most women worked hard all their lives. Roman women could not be heads of families. The father, called in **Latin** the *paterfamilias, "*father of the family," ruled everyone in his household—wife, children, other relatives, servants, and slaves. Roman women had very few legal rights.

Running the home

Although Roman men were in charge legally, most men left the job of running the household to their wives. From the time a newlywed woman entered her new home, which was usually the house of her husband, it became the center of her life. She oversaw the buying of food and supplies, gave pocket money to slaves for good work, or scolded them if they were lazy. She also brought up the children.

Raising the children

Many children of slaves, and children whose parents were too poor to pay for school, never learned to read or write. Wealthier families either sent their children to school, or hired a private tutor to teach in the home. Both girls and boys went to elementary school, but girls left school by the age of thirteen. They stayed at home to help their mother and learning home-management to prepare them for marriage. Boys went on to high school to learn history, arithmetic, and Latin and Greek literature. They could expect to work outside the home, perhaps in government, law, or the army.

The Family at Home

Few Roman children saw their father during the day. He was usually away from home, working or meeting friends. Children seldom went far from their home village or town, though some made visits to relatives, traveling on foot or in wagons.

Home life

Women looked after the house and children, while men were at work. A wealthy woman gave orders to her **slaves,** and to the hired nurse caring for her baby. Some slaves were treated kindly, and were freed as a reward for loyal service. Others were able to save enough money to buy their freedom. A female slave might even marry her master. A freed slave sometimes did well in business and became a prosperous homeowner himself. Other slaves were not so lucky. A bad-tempered master upset by a poor dinner could beat a slave, and there was nothing the slave could do about it.

Most men finished work by mid-afternoon, and husband and wife would dine together, unless the husband had been invited out for the evening. Many women had their own bedrooms, shared with the smaller children. A married woman often shared the home with her husband's mother.

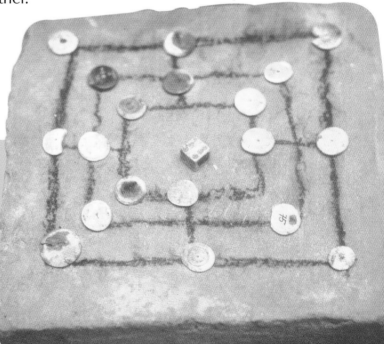

At home, families enjoyed games of different kinds. The Romans particularly liked board games. This gameboard with pieces and dice was found at Vindolanda in northern Britain. It probably belonged to a soldier.

The death of a husband could break up the family home. Some Roman women raised children alone, as single parents, after the deaths of their husbands. However, a **widow** had no right to keep her home unless her husband had left it to her in his **will.** Many widows needed to marry again for security.

Family pets

Many Roman homes had animal residents. Dogs, cats, and caged birds were popular pets. Dogs are often shown on Roman tombstones, and cats too are pictured on **mosaics.** Parrots, imported from Africa and Asia, were sold in markets and people probably taught the birds to "speak" in **Latin.** People returning from foreign lands brought back other more exotic pets, such as tortoises, snakes, and monkeys.

Work and leisure

A Roman home was usually busy. There was always work to be done in the home, or outside in the garden or family vegetable plot. Large houses had piped water, but most people had to fetch water for drinking, cooking, and washing in buckets from a well or public tank. The rich had slaves, but poor people did their own fetching and carrying.

After dinner, the family might gather on a summer evening outside in the garden. In winter, they would sit around the fire by the light of oil lamps. To amuse themselves, people read poetry aloud, played board games such as "Robbers," where you tried to steal other players' pieces, or told stories. They played musical instruments, such as a flute or a stringed lyre, which is a small harp. Children got out their toys—dolls, toy carts, miniature "play-people" made from clay, balls, and rattles.

A mosaic fixed outside a house in Pompeii warned people to "beware of the dog." The Romans kept dogs as pets and for hunting, as well as to guard the family home.

11

Life in the Big City

Rome was the heart of the Roman **Empire.** A million people lived in this city of palaces and **temples,** and its *Forum* was the center of Roman government. **Latin** was the Roman language, but in Rome's streets many other languages were heard because people from all over the Roman world came to the city.

The greatest city of the empire

The finest **architects,** artists, and engineers worked in Rome, to add to its splendors. Every day, people came and went along the city's main roads, the Via Flaminia running north, the Via Latina and Via Appia leading southeast. The Via Ostiensis led to Ostia, the city's port at the mouth of the Tiber River, some 12 miles (20 kilometers) from Rome. Kings, governors, **merchants,** farmers, soldiers, and workers in every trade made their way to Rome. They traveled on horses and donkeys, in carts pulled by **oxen,** and on foot.

Almost every visitor marveled at Rome's size and splendor. Around 350 CE, an official survey shows that the city had 28 libraries, 8 parks, 11 public baths, 10 **aqueducts,** 2 circuses for **chariot** races, and 2 **amphitheaters,** for **gladiator** fights and other shows. There were 144 public toilets, 254 cornmills, and more than 1,000 fountains.

The Forum in Rome was the heart of Roman power. It began as a marketplace. Here were the city's greatest temples, the *Curia* or Senate House, and the Hall of Records or *Tabularium*. There were other forums in Rome but this one, known as the Roman Forum, was the first and most important.

Rich and poor in Rome

Rome's 2,000 richest families lived in the largest and finest private houses. Poorer families lived in about 46,000 apartment buildings, or *insulae*. Some similar buildings can still be seen at Ostia. People living on the top floor of an apartment building had between 100 and 150 stairs to climb. There were no bathrooms, and people either had to go downstairs to use the toilet or use a bucket. From the windows and balconies, **tenants** could gaze down on the street, where beggars, street traders, and trash-collectors mingled with **slaves,** soldiers, lawyers, and businessmen.

Overcrowding and collapse

Apartment buildings were so close together that the writer Martial said he could lean out of his window and shake hands with his neighbor. The ground floor was rented out as stores, and the builders crammed as many rooms as possible on top. Such flimsy buildings often fell down. The lawyer Cicero bought an apartment building, but complained that two shops had fallen down and the walls were cracked so badly that the tenants, and even the mice, had left!

Some of the residents in this apartment block in the port town of Ostia would have been storekeepers, living in rooms above their stores.

Fire!

Emperor Augustus set up Rome's first fire service, with seven brigades of 1,000 *vigiles*, equipped with hand-pumps and buckets. The firefighters could not save the city in 64 CE, when a great fire burned for nine days. Many wooden homes were destroyed. The emperor Nero rebuilt the city with wider streets and more stone buildings. By law, every house was to have fire-fighting equipment, and public water tanks were to be kept filled.

A Roman Town

Across the Roman **Empire,** millions of people lived in towns and cities. Rome was by far the biggest city with its one million people. Roman London, a provincial capital, had at least 50,000 people; Pompeii, a middle-sized seaside town, had around 20,000 **citizens** before its destruction in 79 C.E.

New homes for soldiers

The Romans built new towns wherever they went. Some were founded to provide homes for retired soldiers, like the colony at Corinth in Greece. The Romans destroyed much of Corinth in 146 BCE during their conquest of Greece, but in 44 B.C.E. Julius Caesar decided to build a settlement for retired soldiers there. This meant rebuilding Corinth, which became the capital of Roman Greece.

After they conquered Britain in 43 C.E., the Romans took over the Britons' city of Colchester. **Archaeologists** estimate that the new *colonia* here had about 3,000 ex-soldiers, plus their families— probably 15,000 in all, with newcomers joining them. Many Roman towns were much smaller.

The remains of brick or stone houses give clues as to how many people lived in a town. However, the poorest people probably lived in wooden shacks. Herculaneum was buried by volcanic mud to a depth of 65 feet (20 meters). The mud hardened and preserved the buildings.

The town plan

A typical Roman town was planned on a grid. Pompeii and Herculaneum, so amazingly well preserved, give us our best view into Roman town planning. Pompeii was about 3,900 feet (1,200 meters) long by 2,275 feet (700 meters) wide. It had two main streets, one connecting the north and south gates, and the other running from east to west, towards the sea. Along the smaller streets were rows of houses, stores, and workshops.

Traffic problems

As Roman towns grew, so did traffic congestion. People complained of noise and dust made by carts, farm animals, and construction work. In 45 BCE, new regulations banned all carts from central Rome "between sunrise and the tenth hour," unless they were carrying materials for building temples or public works. **Priests** were allowed to use carts during the "quiet time," and any carts brought into the city at night could be removed by day, empty or filled with animal waste.

Every Roman town had **temples,** bakeries, mills, food stores, bars, and usually a bathhouse, where men and women met to bathe, exercise, and talk with friends. Streets were busy and often dirty or flooded. Visitors to Pompeii can still use its pedestrian crossings—large stones set in the street so that people could step across without getting their feet wet.

Forum and amphitheatre

In Pompeii, as in any Roman town, the *Forum* was where local people ran things. It was a large open space, surrounded by shops and offices, including the council meeting hall. Pompeii's citizens met at the *Forum* to buy and sell goods, make business deals, and argue over the town's affairs. Here too were the law courts, government offices, and most important temples.

Romans liked to be entertained. Even a town the size of Pompeii had an **amphitheater** big enough to hold 12,000 people or more. Crowds packed in to watch **gladiator** fights, or shows with wild animals, mock-battles, and clowns. Local politicians put on shows in the town's amphitheater to win support from the citizens.

A Home in the Country

Most Romans loved the countryside. Their ancestors had been farmers, and farms provided the food and materials on which Rome depended. To get away from it all, rich Romans liked nothing better than to leave the city for the peace and quiet of their country **villa.**

What was a villa?

There were several kinds of villas. To a Roman, a villa could be a family farmhouse, a weekend home, or a huge country estate with hundreds of farmworkers. Seaside holiday homes were also known as villas, and so were some town houses. Wall paintings from Pompeii show elegant seaside villas, from which residents could enjoy the sunshine and gaze out across the Bay of Naples—and at the cone of the volcano Vesuvius.

What a farm villa was like

Lucius Columella, a Roman who wrote about country life around 60 CE, tells us that a villa should have three main parts. They were the owner's house, the house of the farm manager, and the storehouse, which was actually several barns and rooms. In one storeroom, wine and oil would be kept in large pointed jars set into holes in the ground.

This Roman farmer is plowing with oxen. Townspeople thought country people lived simpler, happier lives, and Roman writers often described the joys of country living.

Luxuries and everyday foods

Some villas raised luxury foods, such as snails, **dormice,** peacocks, and fish in ponds. Many southern villas, like the Villa Boscoreale near Pompeii, grew grapes for making wine—most Romans' favorite drink. In northern Europe, villas provided everyday foods such as cereals, fruit, vegetables, and meat to people in local towns.

The main house was often single-storied, though some villas had two floors. There was accommodation for the villa owner and his family, as well as guestrooms for visitors, and a bath suite with hot and cold baths.

Around the main house were other buildings. The farm manager lived in a small house, with his own yard. There were humbler living quarters for the **slaves** who worked in the villa fields and looked after the farm animals. The farm animals were kept in the farmyard with its stables for horses, its cowsheds, pigsties, and chicken runs.

A great farm in Italy

Some villas were very grand indeed. The Italian villa of Settefinestre was built around 75 BCE, possibly for a wealthy family called the Sestii. About 87 miles (140 kilometers) northwest of Rome, this great farm's main activity was growing grapes for wine and olives for oil.

The villa's outer walls had small turrets, which must have made it look very imposing. The main house was 150 Roman feet (44.3 meters) square, and the rooms were decorated with **mosaics** and wall paintings. Built on to this splendid residence was a working area with a toilet big enough for 20 workers, an oil-press, and a room for treading grapes, to squeeze out the juice, to make wine. Besides the main block, Settefinestre villa had at least three walled gardens, what looks like a large pig-house with 27 concrete rooms with feeding troughs, and an orchard.

A Ruler's Palace

Some Roman homes were true palaces. In 1960, a worker digging a trench in Sussex, England, came across some ancient stones. He had unearthed the remains of one of the most remarkable Roman homes. The "palace" at Fishbourne is the biggest Roman house in Britain.

Work by **archaeologists** has revealed just how big the 100-room house was. The outline of about a fourth of its area can be seen. The rest lies buried beneath a modern road and houses.

Decorated walls and floors

Fishbourne once had four sides, or wings, around a central space laid out as formal gardens with trees and hedges. Inside, its halls and rooms would have astonished visitors unused to Roman taste as they walked through a great hallway, flanked by columns. No two rooms appear to have been the same. Walls were first painted in pale background colors such as yellow, and then "framed" pictures of landscapes, plants, animals, and people were painted on top. Most rooms had **mosaic** floors, probably laid by workers brought to England from Gaul or Italy. Central heating came from the **hypocaust,** which sent hot air through spaces beneath the floors and between the walls.

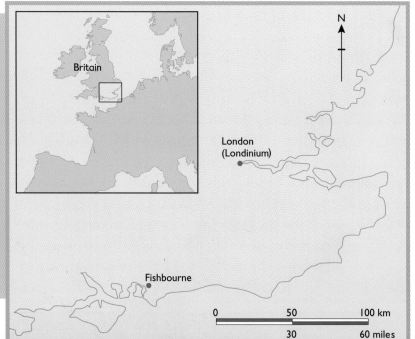

This map shows where the palace at Fishbourne was. It was built near a Roman military camp, set up soon after the invasion of Britain in 43 C.E. It was close to a harbor, to which ships could sail easily from ports elsewhere in Britain and across the sea in Roman Gaul.

Britain

N

London
(Londinium)

Fishbourne

| 0 | 50 | 100 km |
| 30 | 60 miles |

Whose home was it?

This once-splendid building, now protected under a museum roof, must have belonged to an important ruler. The most likely owner is a king named Cogidubnus, who ruled a local people called the Regni in the 1st century CE. His base was probably the town of Noviomagus (Chichester), close to Fishbourne. Cogidubnus helped the Roman invaders who came to Britain in 43 CE, became a Roman **citizen**, and set out to build a home to rival the palaces of the **emperors** in Italy.

The forgotten palace

We know a little about Cogidubnus from the Roman writer Tacitus who says he was a good friend to Rome. Rulers after Cogidubnus went on making improvements to Fishbourne, until the palace burned down shortly before 300 CE. It was never a home again. Many stones were carted away, the garden was overgrown, and Fishbourne lay forgotten for centuries.

The dipping floor

The builders knocked down an earlier Roman-style house (built between 50 and 70 CE) and built a much larger "palace." They did not always get things right. A black and white mosaic floor, made about 75 CE, sank because it was laid on top of an old garbage pit. The builders tried to level the floor with rubble and cement, and laid a new mosaic, the "Cupid on a Dolphin" floor, in about 160 CE. Unfortunately, the floor sank again. People had to get used to a room with a dip in it. In fact, when modern experts lifted and reset this mosaic, they had to put it back in its sunken shape—to flatten it would have meant it no longer fit the room!

The Romans liked mosaic decoration in their homes. The Cupid on a Dolphin mosaic at Fishbourne is made from about 360,000 small pieces of colored stone, called *tesserae*.

A Merchant's House

Trade was important in Roman times, and merchants who did well in business became rich enough to build homes that were among the best in town. From Pompeii, we know a lot about the house of two merchant brothers, who had risen in the Roman world to become leading **citizens** of the town. Theirs is one of the finest houses preserved after the volcano buried the town.

Who were these merchants?

Their names were Aulus Vettius Restitutus and Aulus Vettius Conviva. We know the house belonged to them because their names are on bronze seals in the *atrium*. Bronze is a metal made from copper and tin. The names of the Vettii were also written on the walls outside, in **graffiti** slogans urging voters to support the merchants in town elections.

Like other Romans who had made it from humble beginnings, the Vettii were not ashamed to show off their wealth. They contributed to the cost of public works in Pompeii, and did not skimp on home comforts. In fact, they

The house of the Vettii is in Pompeii. This house has been restored so visitors can see the wall paintings the residents enjoyed so much.

kept the local artists busy decorating their home.

A house full of paintings

As a visitor entered the house, he was greeted by pictures of a cockfight, and what appears to be a picture of a god. In front of the visitor was the *atrium*. Here, as his hosts greeted him, the visitor might notice the two sturdy safes containing the Vettiis' valuables.

Home, sweet home

A house like the Vettii house is an example of what Romans called a *domus*. A *domus* was any private family home, from the modest to the luxurious. It was usually divided into two parts, the *atrium* and the *peristyle*. It provided more roomy living space than the other main kind of Roman dwelling—the *insula*, or tenement building, which housed numerous families.

The rooms opening off the *atrium* were decorated with scenes from Greek and Roman mythology. Among these scenes are pictures of the hero Perseus and the maiden Andromeda, Leander swimming the Hellespont, and Daphne being chased by the god Apollo. Another series of pictures in the *triclinium*, or dining room, shows busy little Cupids, hard at work making wine, practicing archery, making cloth, weighing and beating gold to make jewelry, selling wine, and riding in **chariots.** Other rooms have wall paintings of sea creatures and plants. It was like living in an art gallery.

Servants and garden

From the south side of the *atrium*, steps led to the upper floor of the house. There was a corridor from the "tradesmen's entrance," where goods were delivered, alongside which were a stable and a toilet. The **slave**-servants lived in rooms along the north side of the house. The servants' quarters, the kitchen, and the *peristyle*, an open-air court with columns supporting a canopy for shade, were all preserved so well that restorers have been able to recreate this house. Now it looks much as it did before the volcano Vesuvius erupted in 79 CE.

What Were Homes Made of?

◄▶ ◄▶ ◄▶ ◄▶ ◄▶ ◄▶ ◄▶ ◄▶ ◄▶ ◄▶ ◄▶ ◄▶ ◄▶ ◄▶ ◄▶ ◄▶ ◄

Roman houses were built to last. Styles did not change very much, because most Romans wanted a home that looked "traditional." Many homes stayed in the same family for generations. If more space was required, a homeowner would often add on extra rooms rather than move to a new and bigger house.

Planning the site

A Roman town like Pompeii was planned by **architects,** surveyors, and builders. The architect would draw a plan of the house, and tell the buyer how much it was likely to cost. A rich person might ask for piped water to be laid into a bath-suite big enough for guests, and a study with extra space for his library.

Before building work began, the surveyor would measure the site, using instruments such as the *groma*, a pole with a cross at the top, from the arms of which hung four weighted plumb lines. The plumb lines showed the surveyor that the pole was vertical, an accurate guide to laying out straight lines for walls and streets. Builders also used a kind of spirit level, called a *chorobates*, to check that surfaces such as floors and windowsills were level.

Roman builders' tools include a chisel (center), hammer head (right), and trowel (second from right). They used iron nails (left) and wooden pegs to fasten wood together. The small pyramid-shaped object is a lead plumb bob, which the builder hung from a line to check that a wall was vertical.

The concrete revolution

The Romans made concrete by mixing lime, sand, and water, and adding what builders today call ballast—small stones or rubble. Concrete was not just strong and long lasting; it could be shaped in a mold while still wet, and smoothed to give a plaster-like finish. To make a concrete building look attractive, Roman builders added a coating of polished brick or marble.

Builders at work

The walls and floors of Roman houses were made from blocks of stone, or clay bricks. Bricks were made from wet clay, shaped in molds and either dried in the sun or hardened in a kiln (oven). Stones and bricks were set in mortar (cement), made by mixing burned lime and volcanic ash or sand. Roman builders discovered how to make concrete during the 3rd century B.C.E. and started to build concrete houses—the first in the world.

Cement was used for **mosaic** floors made from patterns of tiny stones, positioned while the cement was still wet. Walls were covered with **plaster,** onto which artists painted friezes (picture-strips) and wall paintings.

Raising the roof

Roman roofs were almost always sloping and made from clay tiles. The standard roof tile was rectangular, with raised edges. Flat tiles were used on floors and walls. Broken tiles ended up in walls, and special hollow tiles were used as pipes to carry hot air from the house's central heating system, or **hypocaust.**

Tiles were made from terra-cotta, a reddish-brown clay mixed with sand, like this tile from a building on Hadrian's Wall in Britain. Slate was also used for roofing, as it is sometimes today.

Furniture and Decoration

Romans liked their homes to look light and cool, with colorful paintings on the **plaster** walls and patterns of **mosaics** on the floors. Rooms were not cluttered with a lot of furniture.

A Roman bedroom was usually small, with just a bed and perhaps a chair and a chest for clothes. People slept on wooden beds sprung with leather straps, and softened by a mattress stuffed with straw or wool. Pillows were filled with anything soft and sweet smelling, such as grass, feathers, wool, and dried herbs. Woolen blankets kept sleepers warm and cozy. Curtains were often hung across doorways, and were rarely used across windows.

Chairs and tables

Chairs were kept for elderly people and guests. Most people sat on wooden stools, or lay down to relax on beds or daycouches. Couches either had ends, but no backs, or had backs like modern sofas. Ornaments were displayed on wooden shelves, and valuables such as jewels were kept in boxes, though in later Roman times cupboards became popular. A poor family made their own wooden stools and tables, but rich Romans spent a small fortune on expensive tables made from marble or silver, inlaid with patterns in **ivory,** tortoiseshell, or rare woods. Tables with a single leg were especially expensive.

A round table like this would have been used for drinks and snacks, and for displaying flowers or ornaments.

Glass is easily broken, so Roman glassware is seldom found in one piece. The Romans learned the skill of glass blowing from Syria. Fine glass like this bowl was found only in rich people's homes. Glass was also used to make jars, bottles, and drinking glasses.

In the dining room or *triclinium*, which means "room with three couches," couches were arranged on three sides of the table. Each couch was long enough for three people to lie on while they ate. Children sometimes had their dinner in the kitchen.

Pictures and ornaments

The Romans decorated floors with colored tile pictures or mosaics. They also put down woven rugs. Poor people's homes had floors of hard-packed mud, with a mat of woven reeds or wool to add a touch of comfort.

Wall paintings of plants, animals, and scenes from old stories were very popular. A rich Roman would be proud of his **busts** and statues—a scholar might have a bust of the Greek philosopher Socrates, to show how serious he was! He might show off a Chinese vase, a Persian rug hung on the wall, or a **Celtic** shield—a trophy from his army service. In pride of place would be masks, or sculpted heads of the family ancestors.

Pictures in Pompeii

Some people in Pompeii liked fantasy worlds on their walls. Wall paintings in houses show landscapes with fantastic-looking buildings. Others preferred big history pictures. A mosaic picture of Alexander the Great in battle is 19.5 feet (6 meters) long.

Heat and Light

Coming from sunny Italy, the Romans liked shade indoors. Very few windows faced the street. People preferred windows to face inwards, so that they could enjoy looking at their garden-courtyard, untroubled by noise from the street outside. Windows had wooden shutters to keep out night air, cold winds, and thieves. Only a few rich people could afford glass windows, though the glass was so thick it did not let much light through.

Lighting the lamps

At night, the Romans lit oil lamps. These were small metal or pottery jars filled with olive oil, into which was dipped a short wool wick. A tablespoon of oil burned for two hours and gave about as much light as a candle. Rich people had elegant lamp stands, from which small lamps hung from chains. Roman candles were made from wax or animal-fat. Candleholders have been found at Pompeii, and large candelabra were used in **temples** and public buildings. You need a lot of candles to light a home, so after sunset Roman rooms must have been quite dark and shadowy.

Heating and the hearth

In Italy, heating was only needed in mid winter. It was a different story in north Britain. When it became chilly, people lit braziers (metal baskets) burning **charcoal** or wood. Fetching fuel and cleaning out the fire were jobs for a **slave.**

In this pottery oil lamp the wick was pushed into the hole in the center. The decoration shows a man driving a chariot. Olive oil was the Romans' most important fuel for burning in lamps. They also made candles, which they fixed in branched holders or candelabra.

The hearth (fireplace) was the center of a Roman home. Early Romans cooked over a fire in an open hearth in the middle of the main room, which became the *atrium*. Later Roman homes had fireplaces set into an outside wall, with a hole or flue for the smoke to escape. Some houses had a separate kitchen to reduce the risk of the main house catching fire. The household fire was such an important symbol of home life that Romans liked to "keep the home fire burning" but they also feared their houses being burned to the ground.

Keep the coal fires burning

The usual fuel for a Roman hypocaust was wood or charcoal, but in Britain coal was also burned. There is evidence of coal burning from at least 20 Roman sites. Coal found at Ely, in eastern England, had been carted or boated from mines in the Forest of Dean over 124 miles (200 kilometers) away.

Central heating by hot air

Wealthy families could afford a central heating system or **hypocaust,** though in many houses this heated only the dining room and baths. The furnace was outside, below ground level, and slaves kept the fire burning with firewood pushed in through a stokehole. The floors of the house were supported by pillars of tiles or stones, so that hot air and smoke from the furnace could circulate freely beneath the rooms. Heat was also channeled up through hollow tiles in the walls, finally escaping through openings in the brickwork.

This picture shows the underfloor arrangement in the dining room of a large house belonging to an army commander serving on Hadrian's Wall in Britain. The pillars held up the floor, and in the space beneath, hot air from the hypocaust kept the soldier's family and guests warm, even in a British winter.

Welcome to the Atrium

Roman homes were designed for the sunny climate of central and southern Italy. Even when forced to make some adjustments for cold, wet climates, Romans liked homes with a Mediterranean feel to them. The main feature of the Roman family house was the *atrium*, which was a "window on the world," open to the sun and sky.

What went on in the atrium?

The *atrium* was the public space of a Roman house. A visitor would be met by a servant as he or she came in from the street entrance. Then the head of the family would welcome them in the *atrium*. Unless they were close friends, or had been invited to dinner, visitors might not see any more of the house.

Instead of windows, this Roman *atrium*, from a house in Pompeii, is lit by sunlight streaming in through the roof opening. The tank in the center collects the rainwater.

The *atrium* was a square
courtyard with an overhanging
roof of tiles. In the middle
of the floor beneath the roof
opening was a marble basin, the
impluvium, into which rainwater
dripped from the roof. Around
the edge of this open space
were alcoves and niches where
people could sit, talk, and have
some privacy if they wanted.
The Romans borrowed the
shape of the *atrium* from
older Etruscan houses.

Lock up your valuables

Rich Romans often kept their
valuables in the *atrium*. To stop
burglars, and to protect their gold
and jewels, they relied on locks
and keys, guard dogs, safes, and
trick strongboxes that would open
only if turned on their sides. In a
Roman lock, the bronze key
turned in the iron lock, the same
way a modern key works. Roman
padlocks had springs to hold the
bolt tight until the key was inserted
to release them.

Business and prayer

The *atrium* was a place of business. It was the house-owner's office,
for dealing with official callers. The *atrium* was also important in Roman
religion, because in it was the **altar** to the family gods—the **Lares.** A small
statue of a Lar, a youthful figure holding a cup and a drinking horn, was
placed there and the family said a prayer to the Lar each morning.

Next to the *atrium* was a room called the *tablinum*, the main living room
that could be curtained off for privacy. Beyond it, reached by a hallway, was
the *peristyle*-garden. Built over the *atrium* and *peristyle* in large houses was
the upper floor, with small rooms used as bedrooms and servants' rooms.

The peristyle and family rooms

The *peristyle* was a pleasant place to relax, away from the public eye.
Leading off this court decorated with columns, open to the sky, and with a
sunlit garden in its center, were various rooms. The *oecus* was an informal
reception room where family friends might sit and chat. The *cubiculae*
were bedrooms. The *alae* were side-halls or cubicles, handy for private
conversations, reading, or dozing. The *triclinium* or dining room was often
designed to let in sunlight through different windows at different seasons.

Entitling

Most Romans, except **slaves,** of course, did most of their work in the morning, so had the afternoons free for leisure and entertaining. For public entertainment, such as plays, **chariot** races, and **gladiator** fights, people went out. At home, people welcomed relatives and friends, entertaining them with food, wine, music, conversation, and various amusements.

Feasts and parties

Even poor Romans might invite friends to share a humble meal, but feasts and parties given by the ruling rich could be very lavish. Many Roman writers criticized rich Romans for over-eating. Stories of wild extravagance should not fool people into thinking that all Romans gorged on delicacies such as roast **dormice** and larks' tongues, drank too much wine, made themselves sick, and then staggered back to the table to eat some more. A few Romans no doubt did behave in this way, but most people did not. While they could shriek for blood when cheering gladiators in the arena, Romans at home were generally very respectable.

A Roman dinner party

Entertaining went on in the dining, reception, or living room, and in the garden. In the Roman dining room, guests arranged themselves around the table on three couches. The meal was served by slaves. Usually three courses were offered, and wine was drunk during and after the meal. A slave might play music to entertain the diners.

Romans lay down to eat, resting on one elbow, though they did have chairs. Three people shared a couch, and nine was the usual number of dinner guests.

This **mosaic** from Pompeii shows street musicians, one playing pan pipes, one playing a tambourine. Performers were hired to give private shows in people's homes.

The Romans did not like to rush their meals. Dinner began around four o'clock in the afternoon and often lasted three hours! It was a time to talk over the events of the day, to exchange news, discuss politics, art, or sport, and tell stories. Parties might go on late into the night, but most evenings Romans went to bed early and rose again at daybreak the next day.

Home entertainment

At home, when the day's work was done, Romans amused themselves. They told stories, read, played games with the children, and sang songs. Men might play dice—many Romans liked to gamble—though "gaming" for money was more usual in taverns.

Leisure

The **Latin** word for "leisure" was *otium*. Its opposite was *negotium*, which meant business. Most Romans enjoyed their leisure time, though one person in Pompeii evidently disapproved of such "time-wasting" because one piece of graffiti found there reads, "This is no place for people who want to relax. Go away, time-waster!"

In a big house or **villa,** the host might pay for professional entertainment for his guests. There might be recitations of poetry by an educated slave or even by the poet, musical items, or a performance by acrobats or dancers. Actors might be hired to put on a short play, perhaps a comedy with jokes written especially for the occasion. As the party wore on, guests would stand up and make speeches thanking the host for his generosity and saying what a fine fellow he was. In reply, the host might recite one of his own poems.

31

In Private

A large house might have bedrooms on the ground floor as well as upstairs. Sometimes husbands and wives shared a bedroom, but as a rule there were separate rooms for men and women. Young children probably slept in the same rooms as their mother, older sisters, aunt, or grandmother. **Slaves** either had their own rooms, slept in storerooms, or bedded down together in a dormitory in the attic of the house.

When they retired to bed, Romans took off their outer clothes and slept in their underwear, or naked if the night was very warm. For a man, underwear meant a **loincloth** and **tunic;** for a woman a short tunic called a *camisia* and linen briefs. The **emperor** Augustus is said to have worn four tunics in bed to keep warm in winter!

Clothing

People kept their clothes in wooden chests and on shelves. A man wore a tunic, with a belt, which reached to the knees. A Roman wore a **toga** for special occasions. The toga was a strip of woolen cloth about five yards (5 meters) long, draped around the body. A toga was hot, and very awkward to wear, so was not normally worn indoors. Most men preferred shorter cloaks or even trousers like the **Celts**.

Indoors, people wore slipper-like sandals, putting on heavier shoes to go out. Romans took their indoor slippers with them when visiting because it was impolite to enter a friend's home wearing outdoor shoes.

All Roman men wore togas. Many statues, such as this one, show men wearing togas, but no one is quite sure how a Roman kept it in place while walking.

Dressing up for the world

In her private room, female slaves would help a wealthy Roman lady dress and get ready to face the world. While a poor woman probably wore the same dress every day, a rich lady might spend some time picking which dress to wear. She would order her maid to curl and pin her hair while she put on her make-up, whitening her face with chalk and darkening her eyelids with ashes.

A close shave

The Roman writer Martial commented on the perils of a visit to his barber, Antiochus. "Those scars on my chin, like the marks on some old boxer's face, were not made by my wife but by the cursed hand and blade of Antiochus," he wrote. The scientist Pliny recommended that a man who was cut while being shaved should apply spiders' webs soaked in vinegar and oil to the wound!

Before going out, a woman put on her *stola*, an ankle-length robe fastened at the shoulder by a brooch. Over it, she wore a long rectangle of cloth called the *palla*. This could be a shawl, a cloak, or a scarf, depending on how it was draped. Some women wore a veil over their head and shoulders. Rich women sent their dirty clothes to the laundry.

Hairstyles

Men and women went out to the hairdresser's, as well as to the baths. Statues and paintings show various Roman hairstyles, but most Roman men had their hair cut short. There were barbers in every town who shaved customers with an iron razor, using only water—no soap or shaving cream. Beards were uncommon until the emperor Hadrian grew a beard, after which beards became more fashionable.

Roman women usually wore their hair long, parted in the middle and rolled up at the back in a bun or "topknot." A head of reddish-brown hair, found in a cemetery at York, England, was wound into a bun held in place by long pins. Women kept their hair in place with long pins, made of silver, cheaper metals such as bronze, or bone. Brushes and combs were made of wood, bone, antler, or **ivory.**

Washing and Bathing

Waking at dawn, a Roman slipped out of bed, used the chamber pot to go the bathroom (emptied later by a **slave**), quickly washed their face and hands in a basin of water, and dressed. It is not clear whether people cleaned their teeth much, though they probably used toothpicks after a meal, and rinsed with mouthwashes to get rid of unpleasant tastes. The gritty flour in Roman bread wore away teeth, but on the whole Roman teeth were healthy—they ate fewer sweet, sticky foods than we do.

Washing up

In the kitchen, washing up was done in bowls, using water but no soap! Metal dishes were cleaned by rubbing them with sand.

Water was brought into town along **aqueducts,** great stone water-channels that the Romans became expert at building. Some of these water-channels were laid in tunnels or across bridges spanning rivers and gorges. Water for Pompeii was brought from 25 miles (40 kilometers) away, and stored in a reservoir, which fed lead tanks around the town. Pipes carried the water to people's homes, and to baths and public fountains.

Water was carried into Roman towns along great aqueducts, like this one in southern France. Called the *Pont du Gard*, it has three tiers of arches crossing the Gard River. Water flowed along it into a reservoir in the town of Nîmes.

Visitors welcome to bathe

The Villa of Julia Felix in Pompeii was one of the biggest houses in the town, with its own baths, and sweat-room, or sauna. It also had an outdoor pool. Originally built for the owner's private use, the baths were later opened to the people of the town. The villa also had a number of workshops which were rented out to local businesses.

Personal hygiene

The reason why Romans did not take baths in the morning was that people usually visited the public baths later in the day. Romans did not need bathrooms at home. Public bathing was made popular by the mother of the **emperor** Augustus, who encouraged her rich friends to join her at the public bathhouse. A few very rich people enjoyed the luxury of a private bathroom and used toilets flushed by piped water from a tank. In the country, where public baths were too far from home, a guest staying at a **villa** could enjoy the comforts of central heating and hot and cold water piped to the bath-suite. In most poor homes, water had to be fetched and stored in a stone trough or in buckets made of wood or leather.

Many Romans used outdoor one-seat or two-seat toilets. Public toilets, and those built in forts for soldiers, were communal—a plank with a row of seat-holes over a ditch. The Romans did not have toilet paper, but used sponges on sticks. They rinsed the sponges in water flowing along a channel cut into the floor.

The Romans did not use soap for washing. At the baths, they poured out olive oil from a flask and rubbed the oil into the skin. Then they scraped off the mixture of oil, dirt, and sweat using a curved scraper like this, called a *strigil*.

The Kitchen

The usual Roman stove was a stone table on which small fires of glowing **charcoal** burned in holes. Food was cooked in pots, pans, and basins resting on metal grills placed over the burning charcoal. Ovens were made of brick, and heated by a fire lit inside the oven. When the fire was really hot, the ashes were raked out, and the food—bread, meat or pastry—was put into the oven to cook.

Kitchen tools included knives, ladles, spoons, strainers, choppers, and **pestles and mortars** for crushing herbs or nuts. For soups and stews, cooks hung large metal pots from chains over the fire. When a clay pot became too dirty, even after scraping, it was thrown away.

Many poor people had no kitchen of their own. They bought take-out food such as sausages, cheese, fried fish, and boiled eggs from stalls in the street. For a small fee, the local baker would also cook meat or pies in his oven.

Breakfast, lunch, and dinner

A Roman breakfast was simple, usually a cup of water and bread and honey. Lunch was a snack: perhaps bread and cheese, eggs, salad, and fruit. People drank red and white wines, usually mixed with water.

A modern reconstruction of a Roman kitchen is based on **archaeologists'** finds. Roman cooking pots and pans were made of pottery and bronze. On the right is the stove, with a pot on the grill, and space in the arch beneath for fuel.

By four o'clock in the afternoon, people were ready for dinner. There might be shellfish, sliced eggs, and salad to begin with. This was followed by meat dishes, including hare, pork, beef, goat, lamb, fish, pigeon, chicken, or peacock. For dessert, they would have fruit, nuts, and honey cakes, and as a treat, ice cream made with ice from the mountains. Poor families seldom feasted on such treats. They made do with bread, eaten with pea or bean soup, and porridge.

Saucy cooking

Romans smothered their food with sauces, the favorite being a fishy sauce called *garum*, made chiefly of anchovies or tuna. The sauce often hid the real taste of the food. The cookery writer Apicius wrote at the end of one of his recipes that because the sauce was so rich, "no-one at table will know what he is eating."

Cutlery and tableware

The Romans did not use forks. They picked up food with their fingers, and wiped the plate with hot bread rolls. **Slaves** would bring bowls of water and towels for people to wash their hands between courses.

Food was often served in dishes made from a popular red pottery called Samian ware. Glass was expensive, so olive oil and wine were kept in large pottery jars called *amphorae.* In a grand house, food might be served on silver or pewter (a tin-like metal) plates. Poorer people ate off wooden or pottery dishes.

Seafood was a speciality in seaside towns such as Pompeii, which had a fish-sauce factory. This **mosaic** from Pompeii shows some of the sea creatures such as fish, octopus, squid, and lobster, caught in the Mediterranean Sea and sold to diners in the town.

The Garden

The Romans loved gardens. In a town house, the *peristyle* was the family's favorite summer place, with its shrubs and flowers and rippling fountain. Romans grew potted plants in the *atrium* too, and even poor families living in city apartments tended flowerpots and window boxes.

Many townspeople had a patch of land outside the town walls, called a *hortus*. They grew olive and nut trees, as well as vegetables such as cabbage, cucumber, and lettuce. They also grew plants like onions and garlic, and herbs such as rosemary, lavender, thyme, and mint, used for cooking and medicines. Romans liked roses, lilies, and violets, not just for the flowers' beauty, but also to decorate the **altars** of their household gods.

The lucky gardener

The Roman poet Virgil wrote about the pleasures of gardening. One of his verses describes an old man who grows vegetables in a small patch among the brambles, "coming home late every evening, loaded with home-grown feasts." The garden was not just a place of peace and quiet, away from the noise of the town. It was also a useful source of fresh vegetables and fruit.

Shown here is the House of Venus in Pompeii. It takes its name from the painting of the goddess Venus riding on a seashell on the garden wall. Romans liked painted walls to add interest to the enclosed garden. The family rooms opened onto the garden, and the roof with its columns gave shade from the hot summer sun.

By 100 CE a more formal kind of garden had become fashionable in Rome. There were wide paths for strolling along between trimmed hedges. Roman hedges have been recreated by planting box shrubs along the lines of Roman gardeners' trenches found by **archaeologists**. Formal gardens had stone seats, statues, and fountains fed with water from underground concrete pipes. Herbs scented the air, and ivy was trained around wooden posts and twined around statues of gods. From Pompeii, archaeologists have found post holes and root cavities showing where trees and vines were planted in corners of gardens, for shade, and trained over wooden supports.

Plants wherever the Romans went

The Romans took their favorite plants with them to new lands. For example, they took to Britain fruit trees such as pears and cherries, and vegetables new to the country such as carrots, asparagus, lettuce, radishes, and turnips. They also introduced stinging nettles to eat as a vegetable and to make a hair tonic for balding men.

The house of Loreius Tiburtinus in Pompeii (shown here) had a garden with a trellis, a **temple,** and a stream flowing through it. Tiburtinus was a wealthy man, a **priest** of the Temple of Isis. Worshippers of this Egyptian **goddess** believed water was a symbol of life.

Family Worship

Romans worshiped at home, as well as at **temples.** They believed in powerful household **spirits,** which protected the home, as well as in great gods like the sky god Jupiter; Mars, god of war; and Ceres, **goddess** of the harvest. The Romans borrowed many of their gods from the Greeks (Jupiter was the Greek Zeus, for example), and later took other gods from religions they heard about in foreign countries. For a time, the **emperor** himself was worshiped as a god. By the 300s CE, many people in the Roman **Empire** had turned to Christianity.

Spirits watching over homes

The Romans believed that spirits were everywhere: in the fields, woods, streams, and the home. These supernatural beings watched over everyday activities such as cooking and eating. On the walls of Roman houses you can still see small **shrines,** looking like miniature temples. These were special places for giving thanks to the **Lares** or household guardians to whom the family made gifts of food, drink, or flowers. Vesta watched over the hearth, and was offered food and drink before the family began the main meal of the day. The **Penates** guarded the storeroom, and two-faced Janus watched the comings and goings through the door.

A father led his family in religious ceremonies at home to seek help from these spirits. The family gathered to pray at the shrine every morning, and on special days they put out gifts of food and wine for the spirits. The father would make a *"libation"*—pouring liquid offerings from a bowl onto the sacrificial fire burning on the **altar.**

This *lararium,* a shrine to the household gods, or Lares, is in the House of the Vettii in Pompeii. The family *genius* is the middle figure, with two Lares on either side. Below is a protective snake.

This **mosaic** from the Roman **villa** at Hinton St Mary in Dorset, England was made about 350 C.E. It shows the first two letters of Christ's name, in Greek, so was evidently made for a Christian family.

Guardians of the family

When a child was born, the parents and relatives said prayers and set out a table of food for the gods to ensure the protection of the new baby. A special "guardian angel" of the family was the father's *genius*, pictured either as a snake or as a young man. A woman had her own spirit-guardian, called a *juno*. Romans also believed that they were watched over by the spirits of dead ancestors, who were called the *manes* or "kindly ones." Important families kept wax masks or portraits of their ancestors in the house.

Christians at home

The first Roman Christians were persecuted because they refused to worship the emperor as a god. Like other small cults, Christians met secretly in each other's homes. For some time this was dangerous, and Christians risked being arrested and put to death. The emperor Constantine (*c.*280–337) became a Christian and by the end of the 300s CE Christianity had become the official religion of Rome.

Superstitions

No Roman would do anything important, such as getting married or setting out on a long journey, without consulting an astrologer or fortune-teller. Roman **priests** would examine the insides of dead animals in the belief that "signs" would show what was about to happen. Sometimes people ran home with startling stories of "strange omens"— someone had seen an ox walking up three flights of stairs, or a wolf snatching a soldier's sword! To a Roman, such omens meant something awful was about to happen.

How Do We Know about Roman Homes?

◁▷ ◁▷ ◁▷ ◁▷ ◁▷ ◁▷ ◁▷ ◁▷ ◁▷ ◁▷ ◁▷ ◁▷ ◁▷ ◁▷ ◁

We know about the Romans from what they left behind. They built everywhere they went. Few people in history left so much evidence of their achievements.

Archaeological evidence

Many Roman towns, forts, and villas have been excavated by **archaeologists.** The most famous Roman town is Pompeii, in Italy. Finds made here and at other sites reveal how Roman houses were built, and what Roman home life was like.

What happened to Pompeii

On August 24, 79 CE, the Roman writer Pliny the Younger wrote that "my mother pointed out to Uncle an odd-shaped cloud." The cloud was a column of smoke, ash, and lava from the erupting volcano Vesuvius. On that day, disaster struck Pompeii and its neighboring towns of Stabiae and Herculaneum, nestling beside the Bay of Naples in Italy, in the shadow of the great volcano.

It was a catastrophe. Thousands of Romans died, many suffocated by poisonous gases. Others fled. Pompeii was buried by ash over four yards

A painting shows people fleeing as Pompeii is buried by ash and lava from the volcano Vesuvius. This painting is English, and dates from 1820.

(4 meters) deep. The town was never rebuilt. It lay forgotten until the 1700s CE when people began to dig into the mud and ash, and found evidence of the buildings and streets beneath. Today much of Pompeii has been uncovered so that visitors walking through the streets can easily imagine themselves back in Roman times.

What Pompeii tells us about Roman homes

Pompeii gives us our clearest picture of how a Roman town was laid out, and what it was like inside a Roman house, with its *atrium,* family rooms, and *peristyle* garden. We can see how extra rooms were added, how decorations became more sophisticated, and how wealthy citizens transformed old vegetable plots into Greek-style courtyard gardens. Above all, Pompeii is rich in wall paintings, so well preserved that they tell us much about Roman home life and art. There are also revealing examples of **mosaics** and sculpture.

A home life not so very strange

In this book, we have seen how the Romans made the home the center of their family lives, in the city or the country. They made few changes in the styles of their houses, adapting the basic design to suit changing times and family fortunes. Roman building techniques, seen in roads, forts, and aqueducts, were just as impressive in the home.

At home, Romans did what people everywhere have done, and still do—they cooked, cleaned, ate, slept, played, talked, laid around, entertained, and shared family pleasures. Today we may not believe in family spirits guarding the door, and we may watch TV rather than tell stories by the light of oil lamps. Yet in many ways, home life has not really changed much in over 2,000 years.

43

Timeline

B.C.E.

753	The city of Rome is founded.
c.510	The Romans revolt against Etruscan rule.
200	Rome by now rules all Italy. The Surgeon's House in Pompeii is built around this time, or earlier.
146	Greece and Macedonia become Roman provinces. The Romans copy Greek styles of housebuilding and decoration.
100	Romans use concrete for building.
75	The **Villa** of Settefinestre in Italy is built.
46	Julius Caesar introduces a new calendar for the Roman world.
44	Julius Caesar is murdered.
27	Augustus becomes the first **emperor** of Rome.

C.E.

19	*Pont du Gard* aqueduct is built by Marcus Agrippa.
20	Marcus Gavius Apicius, the famous cook, is alive.
62	An earthquake damages houses in Pompeii, but people rebuild them.
64	A large fire destroys many houses in Rome.
70	Work is in progress on Fishbourne Palace, in Britain.
79	Vesuvius erupts, and buries the Roman towns of Pompeii and Herculaneum.
100	Formal gardens are popular in Rome.
101–107	The Romans conquer Dacia, and the **empire** reaches its greatest size.
c.130	Ptolemy draws the first reasonably accurate maps of the known world.
170	Settfinestre villa in Italy falls on hard times and is abandoned.

212	Most people living in the Roman Empire (except **slaves**) can become citizens.
300	Around this date, Fishbourne Palace burns down.
364	The Roman Empire is divided into separate empires, East (Rome) and West (Constantinople).
378	The last great battle of the Roman legions occurs, when Rome is defeated at Adrianople by the Goths.
476	The last Roman emperor in the West is overthrown by invading Goths.

More Books to Read

Barron's Educational Editorial Staff. *Roman Life*. New York: Barron's Educational Series, Inc., 1998.

Chapman, Gillian. *The Romans*. Chicago: Heinemann Library, 1998.

Dargie, Richard. *A Roman Villa*. Austin, Tex: Raintree Steck-Vaughn Publishers, 2000.

Ganeri, Anita. *The Ancient Romans*. Austin, Tex.: Raintree Steck-Vaughn Publishers, 2000.

MacDonald, Fiona. *I Wonder Why Romans Wore Togas: And Other Questions about Ancient Rome*. New York: Houghton Mifflin Company, 1997.

Martell, Hazel Mary. *Roman Town*. Danbury, Conn.: Franklin Watts, 1998.

Sheehan, Sean and Patricia M. Levy. *Rome*. Austin, Tex: Raintree Steck-Vaughn Publishers, 1999.

Shuter, Jane. *The Ancient Romans*. Chicago: Heinemann Library, 1998.

Glossary

altar table or other special place for making religious offerings

amphitheater large circular stadium, with an arena or sanded area in the middle

amphora pottery jar used to store wine and oil

aqueduct pipe or bridge-like structure for carrying water into towns

archaeologist expert on the past who studies objects and evidence underground or beneath the sea

architect person who designs buildings

bust image made in stone, metal, or clay of a person's head

Celtic belonging to a Celt. Celts were European peoples fought by the Romans.

charcoal "cooked" wood burned as a fuel for stoves and fires

chariot two-wheeled cart drawn by a pair of horses

citizen Roman man entitled to vote in elections and serve in the legions

dormouse a type of rodent used for food

emperor supreme ruler of Rome

empire large area with many peoples living under rule of an emperor

gladiator trained professional fighter who fought in the Roman arena

goddess female god

graffiti wall-writing

graft to bind a cutting of one tree onto another, so that the two grow together

hypocaust Roman hot-air central heating system

inscription writing cut into wood or stone, usually on a gravestone

ivory hard, creamy-white material from elephant's tusks, used for carving

Lares spirits of the house, in Roman religion

Latin language spoken by Romans

loincloth simple form of underwear, a strip of cloth wound around the waist and between the legs

mosaic decoration used on wall and floors, using small stones to make pictures and patterns

oxen cattle used to pull plows and carts

penates spirits of the family storeroom, in Roman religion

pestle and mortar bowl and hand-held crusher used in the kitchen

philosopher person who studies and thinks about the meaning of life

plaster mixture of gypsum or lime and water, used to coat walls

priest person in charge of religious practices; in Roman times priests looked after temples

republic form of government in early Rome, with elected officials, not a king

shrine place thought to be holy, where some religious object is kept

site in archaeology, place where finds about the past have been discovered, often by digging

slave servant who was not free and who belonged to a master

spinning twisting fibers together to make thread

spirit supernatural being

temple building for religious worship

tenant person who rents a home (an apartment or a house) from the owner, known as the landlord

thatched roof made out of straw

toga Roman garment, like a loosely folded cloak

tunic long shirt-like garment

villa country farm-estate or country house

weaving making cloth or rugs by intertwining threads

widow woman whose husband has died

will instructions left by a person to arrange the sharing of his or her possessions after death

Index